SPOTLIGHT ON
IMMIGRATION AND MIGRATION

# NEW JOBS, NEW OPPORTUNITIES

BRITISH IMMIGRANTS ARRIVE IN AMERICA (1830s–1890s)



Pilar Alvarez

PowerKiDS press.

NEW YORK

Published in 2016 by The Rosen Publishing Group, Inc.
29 East 21st Street, New York, NY 10010



Editor: Sarah Machajewski
Book Design: Samantha DeMartin

Photo Credits: Cover, p. 11 Everett Historical/Shutterstock.com; p. 4 Rischgitz/Hulton Archive/Getty Images; pp. 5, 15, 17, 21 courtesy of Library of Congress; p. 7 (spinning jenny) Hulton Archive/Hulton Archive/Getty Images; p. 7 (steam engine) conrado/Shutterstock.com; pp. 8–9 Heritage Images/Hulton Archives/Getty Images; p. 10 Library of Congress/Archive Photos/Getty Images; p. 13 Print Collector/Hulton Archive/Getty Images; p. 14 scott conner/Shutterstock.com; p. 19 DEA Picture Library/De Agostini Picture Library/Getty Images; p. 22 Alberto Masnovo/Shutterstock.com.

Cataloging-in-Publication Data

Alvarez, Pilar.
New jobs, new opportunities: British immigrants arrive in America (1830s–1890s) / by Pilar Alvarez.
p. cm. — (Spotlight on immigration and migration)
Includes index.
ISBN 978-1-5081-4090-0 (pbk.)
ISBN 978-1-5081-4091-7 (6-pack)
ISBN 978-1-5081-4093-1 (library binding)
1. British Americans — History — 19th century — Juvenile literature. 2. British Americans — Economic conditions — 19th century — Juvenile literature. 3. Immigrants — United States — History — 19th century — Juvenile literature. I. Alvarez, Pilar. II. Title.
E184.B7 A48 2016
973'.0421—d23

Manufactured in the United States of America

CPSIA Compliance Information: Batch #BW16PK: For further information contact Rosen Publishing, New York, New York at 1-800-237-9932.

# CONTENTS

# THE BRITISH COME TO THE UNITED STATES

European explorers began arriving in North America in the late 15th century. By the 1600s, many European nations had established colonies in the so-called New World. Since then, what's today known as the United States has attracted millions of **immigrants** to its lands.

Many early immigrants came for religious or political freedom. Others came for adventure or money. During the 1800s, many people who immigrated to the United States came to find work. Between 1820 and 1860, about 4 million immigrants came to the United States from Europe. More than half were from Great Britain.

The British immigrated to escape **famines**, overpopulation, and poor living and working conditions. After 1830, they also came because of the Industrial Revolution. This was a time when new manufacturing processes changed society from having an economy based on agriculture to having one based on factories.

The Industrial Revolution began in Britain around 1760. When it reached the United States, it led to factories and the growth of cities.

# EASY AND EFFICIENT

The invention of machines during the Industrial Revolution caused many agricultural communities to become focused on manufacturing. This happened in Britain and the United States. Before **industrialization**, Britain's economy was based on farming. However, this changed with inventions such as the steam engine and the spinning jenny, which allowed several threads to be spun at once.

Because of the Industrial Revolution, goods that were once made by hand could now be produced with machines, which meant they became less expensive to make and buy. Although that was a positive change, there were negative changes, too. Many farmers lost their jobs. They had to move to the cities to find work. Factories were built to create machine parts, **textiles**, and other goods. Soon, cities were overcrowded, and jobs were hard to come by.

SPINNING JENNY

Inventions such as the steam engine and spinning jenny made tasks easier and more **efficient**.

STEAM ENGINE

# CROSSING THE OCEAN FOR OPPORTUNITY

Britain's population grew rapidly during the Industrial Revolution. It doubled between 1750 and 1800. With its limited land and **resources**, Britain couldn't produce enough food to match its population growth.

Many people, including farmers who had fallen on hard times, moved to cities to find work in factories or mills.

If they had little money, they were forced to live in tenement housing. Tenement houses were small, crowded, and run-down buildings that housed several families.

Britain's food supply suffered during this time because of **droughts**. Famines caused foods such as potatoes and grains to become scarce. By 1830, people were leaving Britain in large numbers to seek better opportunities in the United States.

Many immigrants sailed to the United States on ships that left from Liverpool, England, which was a busy port town.

# NOT ENOUGH WORKERS

Though the Industrial Revolution started in the 18th century, it really took hold in the United States in the late 1800s and early 1900s. The United States had plenty of natural resources, such as coal and iron ore, which were needed for manufacturing. New power supplies, such as steam power and electricity, made production more efficient. Power plants, including electrical plants, were built to meet this need.

There was no shortage of land on which to build factories or towns in which workers could settle. Americans **migrated** from the country to find work in factories. However, America's industries had grown so quickly there weren't enough workers to fill the jobs. Companies began advertising in Britain to **lure** workers to the United States.

The poster on page 10, which was probably created after the waves of British immigrants arrived in the United States, tells people of the better life they could find in America.

# TRAVELING BY STEAMSHIP

Immigrants sailing from Britain made the journey on steamships. Steam engines allowed ships to make the voyage across the Atlantic Ocean more quickly and easily than before. A journey that once took six weeks could now be made in only two weeks.

Many British immigrants were skilled workers and had money to pay for their tickets, but some had to save for several years to afford the trip. They hoped to make money when they arrived in the United States.

The journey from Britain to the United States wasn't easy. Ships were often crowded and dirty. Once the ship reached American ports, immigrants had to register at an immigration station. Castle Garden in New York was the first immigration station in the United States. It opened in 1855.

Immigrants carrying their life's possessions arrive at an immigration station in New York City.

# PLENTIFUL OPPORTUNITIES

While families often immigrated together, many immigrants from Britain were single men. They hoped to use their skills to make money. Their skills weren't in demand anymore in Britain. However, there were many opportunities for such people to begin businesses and do well in the United States.

Samuel Slater was one such person. He was a British man who had specialized knowledge in **technology**. He arrived in Pawtucket, Rhode Island, in 1789, and established the first cotton mill in the United States. He hired entire families, including children, to work in his mill.

Less-skilled British immigrants hoped to find work in already existing factories, mills, and mines. Others dreamed of owning farms, just as they had before the Industrial Revolution.

SLATER'S MILL

The United States had plenty of unsettled land, which created many opportunities for building factories and farms.

# WHERE DID IMMIGRANTS SETTLE?

Many British immigrants who came to the United States settled in the New England area. This was because this area had many textile factories, and British immigrants were often skilled in this trade. Merrimack Manufacturing, which was located in Lowell, Massachusetts, was a textile mill that employed immigrant workers.

Towns in Massachusetts, such as Bedford, New Bedford, and Lawrence, had growing textile industries. Populations of immigrant workers grew along with them. Town records from Lawrence, Massachusetts, show that about 6,000 Irish and 2,000 British immigrants lived there by 1860.

Like other immigrant groups, British immigrants settled in cities near the ports through which they entered the United States. Immigrants who wanted to farm moved further inland, where there were stretches of available land.

This young girl works as a spinner in a factory in Fall River, Massachusetts.

# BUSY AND LIVELY CITIES

The steel and textile industries grew to be very big in the United States because of the Industrial Revolution. Steel and textile factories were usually located in big cities, such as New York, Pittsburgh, Boston, and Chicago. Raw **materials** could be brought to the factories on the new and improved roads and railroads.

New industry meant life in the United States' big cities was busy and lively. The cities had large populations of available workers. Many of the British immigrants who came during the United States' Industrial Revolution settled here because chances of finding work were good.

What kind of work did British immigrants migrate for? They often found work in factories that produced nails, railroad tracks, and gun parts. Many British people found work in textile factories that produced clothing, knit stockings, and shoes.

This 1885 drawing shows carpenters at a factory in Chicago, Illinois. Lumber, or wood, was an important material used in manufacturing.

# WORKING CONDITIONS IN THE FACTORIES

The way people worked changed greatly because of the Industrial Revolution. Before, skilled tradesmen were needed to create products by hand. This included clothes, tools, and furniture. Even machine parts were created by hand. These parts needed careful work. The work was expensive, took a long time, and only produced small numbers of the product at a time.

With industrialization, new machines were invented that allowed products to be made in large numbers. British workers who were skilled tradesmen before now only needed to be skilled enough to operate machines. Many workers found the **repetitive** tasks boring. Workers also faced poor working conditions. Factories were dirty and unsafe. Workers labored six days a week, often for as long as 14 hours a day, for low wages.

British immigrants were among the first to experience the poor working conditions in America's new factories. By the 1900s, people were working to **reform** labor practices to make them better.

# SUCCESS IN THE UNITED STATES

The period from 1830 to 1890 was a time of great change in the United States. It was also a time of change for many immigrants coming from Britain. They left their homeland in search of work and a better way of life.

The Industrial Revolution allowed **enterprising** people to do well. Anyone with an idea and a willingness to work hard could make it in the United States. However, the road to success was not easy, especially for immigrants. They were strangers in a new land. Many worked long, hard hours for little pay. They lived in small, run-down apartments. However, their patience paid off, and many British immigrants were able to make a good life for themselves. By leaving Britain behind, they were able to find success in the United States.

# GLOSSARY

**drought:** A long period of little rainfall and the lack of water it brings.

**efficient:** Working in a well-organized way with little waste.

**enterprising:** Having or showing resourcefulness.

**famine:** An extreme shortage of food.

**immigrant:** A person who comes to live permanently in a new land.

**industrialization:** The process of developing industries on a large scale.

**lure:** To draw someone to something by offering some sort of benefit or reward.

**material:** The matter from which something is made.

**migrate:** To move from one place to another.

**reform:** To make changes to something in order to make it better.

**repetitive:** Happening over and over again.

**resources:** A country's means of supporting itself, such as its land, minerals, or other property.

**technology:** The way people do something using tools and the tools that they use.

**textile:** Cloth.

# INDEX



# PRIMARY SOURCE LIST

Page 5. Portland Star Match Factory. Created by Geo. H. Walker & Co. Lithography. ca. 1860–1880. Now kept at the Library of Congress Prints and Photographs Division, Washington, D.C.

Page 17. Spinner. Created by Lewis Wickes Hine. June 1916. Photograph. Now kept at the Library of Congress Prints and Photographs Division, Washington, D.C.

Page 21. Lawrence, Massachusetts, strikers parading in New York City. Created by Bain News Service. 1911. Photograph. Now kept at the Library of Congress Prints and Photographs Division, Washington, D.C.

# WEBSITES

Due to the changing nature of Internet links, PowerKids Press has developed an online list of websites related to the subject of this book. This site is updated regularly. Please use this link to access the list: www.powerkidslinks.com/soim/brit